Bullets For Life

J. T. Deeman

ISBN: 1453703918
EAN-13: 9781453703915

Printed in the United States

CONTENTS

introduction

There are many things I think of throughout the week that make me slap my forehead and say, "I really need to teach this to my boys." Then those things disappear from my mind, often quite quickly. So I've taken to writing notes to myself from time to time. That's what this book is, a compilation of those notes. I feel like I'm a bit behind the eight ball on this because my oldest son is 16, almost 17, and he will be out of the house soon. There's still so much I should be telling him, I think. Maybe this book will be a step in the right direction.

general Life

- Try to do what you like in life, and if you can figure out how to make a living from doing it, so much the better.

- If something interests you, pursue it early on.

- Sometimes you just have to turn off the noise.

- Shade is good.

- Much of the world's actions won't stand up to common sense.

- You are not invulnerable, and you won't really believe this until you are 50 or older.

- When you think you've embarrassed yourself irrevocably, give it a day or two. By that time, no one will remember.

- Beware the plodding existence bubble. By the time you realize you are in it, you will have lost the energy of youth.

- Dreading something you have to do but haven't done yet makes it seem worse than it really is.

- Most sales aren't.

- It's often difficult to time when to get in the game and when to get out. Knowing when to get in is less important than knowing when to get out.

- Don't vote for candidates just to ensure a certain party wins. Vote for candidates who most closely reflect your values and principles.

- Always be more interested in truth than spin.

- Understand that there are people out there who have the ability to make lies seem like truth.

- Don't believe what politicians say. Watch what they do, how they vote.

- Most people have an agenda.

- If you think you are humble, then you probably aren't.

- Don't confuse humility with being a doormat.

- It's often easier to say "yes" than it is to say "no." That doesn't mean you should.

- People will try to justify all manner of bad behavior. They aren't interested in decency or modesty.

- Human beings were made for work. Perpetual leisure kills the spirit, dulls the mind.

- Change is something you'll have to get used to.

- You can adapt to almost any situation.

- Everyone will ask you for money. No one will offer it to you without wanting something in return. Except maybe parents. Maybe.

- Just because something is legal doesn't make it ethical or right.

- There will be times when it's better to do nothing at all, say nothing at all.

- Don't forget to say, "Thank you."

practical

- When tightening screws or nuts, remember - righty tighty lefty loosey

- Be handy enough to replace a light switch or the workings in a toilet tank.

- Keep a few nonurgent, unfinished projects handy. Don't let them rule you.

- When faced with an overwhelming task, break it down into smaller pieces and tackle those pieces one at a time.

- Don't make important decisions based on feelings.

- Setting priorities prevents activity mayhem.

- Don't overplan your day.

- Do one thing at a time. When you are finished, move on to the next.

- Do the hard things first. Then the easy ones won't seem as daunting.

- Learn how to troubleshoot computer problems and fix them yourself. It can save you a bunch of time and money.

- When setting up home theater/sound systems, it's all about signal flow.

- Using the right tool will make the job easier.

- Things you should know about your car: how to jump start it, how to change a tire, how to change a battery, how to replace windshield wipers, how to check fluid levels and replenish them. Beyond these things, any repairs you can do on your vehicle will be a plus.

- When you get a good idea, write it down.

- If you change your oil every 5000 miles, then your odometer becomes an easy reminder.

- Don't be taken in by flashy advertising.

- We've lost a lot of knowledge as technology has grown. Spend some time in the woods with just a compass and knife.

- Much of nature is edible. Some of it is poisonous. Know the difference.

- You can do with much less than you think you can.

- A job is just an economical contract to ensure cash flow. A career is a job with an attitude.

- If you marry a packrat, make sure you have a lot of storage space.

- Your attitude will affect those around you.

- Know how to balance a checkbook. Do it monthly. Early on it will seem pointless, but you'll eventually come to see the value of it.

- Sometimes you just have to break down and have some fun.

- Don't envy those who have more than you. Help those who have less.

Love, sex & relationships

- People aren't near as interested in you as they are themselves.

- The person who asks questions controls the conversation.

- Your children need you.

- Your wife needs you.

- Niceness and attentiveness will lead to far more sex than whining ever did.

- Sometimes you have to fake affection.

- Some perfumes will drive you crazy. Others won't. I don't know why.

- Sometimes it will be difficult to say, "I love you." Say it anyway. She needs it more than you.

- There will be moments in your marriage when you will wonder if you married the wrong person. Those moments will pass. Don't make any relationship decisions during those moments.

- Love comes with many feelings, but it isn't a feeling. It's a mindset, a commitment.

- The person you marry should be someone you can't picture living without for the rest of your life.

- It's true what they say - if you want to know what a girl will be like in 30-40 years, get to know her mother.

- The person who sees you at your worst and still loves you is worth holding on to.

- Some relationships just don't work out. You may think that it's a match made in heaven, but she doesn't. Or vice versa. You may do something foolish while experiencing the pain of a breakup. Just try not to do something you will regret.

- Infatuation is fun and exciting, but it's not love.

- Women don't really care if you are able to defeat the 50th level boss in a video game.

- Sometimes you need time apart from each other.

- Absence makes the heart grow fonder for a while. After that, there's no guarantee.

- Everyone knows what attracts men: women. We have yet to figure out what attracts women.

- The way a woman thinks and what she does will frustrate you to no end. Just smile and say, "Yes, dear."

- No matter what they say, dating is the process of searching for a spouse. It's not necessary to swing at the first pitch.

- There's never a perfect time to get married or have children. Don't worry about it, it will all seem perfect when you look back at it.

- Men are aroused by visual stimulation. Women are aroused by emotional stimulation. It's a crazy dance.

- Women need affection to feel sexy. Men need sex to feel affectionate. God is a real practical joker.

- It's true - opposites do attract.

- Love at first sight? Not really. It's called attraction. Love takes a lot of time.

- You will be better off marrying someone who shares the same spiritual principles.

- Opposite personalities in a relationship can be frustrating. But they can also round out and temper the union.

- Your children will learn much from you when you least realize it. Be careful.

spiritual

- People have a huge hole in their lives. They try to fill that hole with all sorts of things, food, drugs, alcohol, sex, things, money, status. Filling the hole would make them happy. The only effective filler is Jesus.

- God made human bodies in such a way as to experience pleasure while fulfilling that which is necessary to live and propagate the species. In the proper framework, it's all good and to be encouraged.

- A relationship with God is like a relationship with people. You have to get to know each other. Since God already knows everything about you....

- Know where you stand and stand where you know. There will be a reckoning.

- There's one Bible - you think there'd be one doctrine. Not if man has anything to say about it.

- Power struggles in the church? Very possible, very real.

- Where cultures are economically thriving, God becomes less relevant to them.

- Science is the new Tower of Babel.

- Ecclesiastes is a great book. Read it many times.

- You need to know the Bible well enough that you aren't taken in by false prophets, teachers and preachers.

- Be wary of popular churches.

- *What would Jesus do?* is often spouted by those who have no idea. You'd be better asking, *What did Jesus do?* and *What would Jesus have me do?* If you don't know, read the Bible and pray.

- Find a way to take part in the mission of your church.

- Many people pray to God for a life of ease. What they should be praying for is strength and guidance.

- There are attributes of God you may apprehend, but you'll never really comprehend until you have left this life.

- Anything you do in the service of others can be a ministry.

- Christianity is a marathon, not a sprint.

- Prayer doesn't have to be on your knees with your head bowed and eyes closed. It can be while driving, at work, in moments of silence anywhere.

- If someone pops into your head from out of the blue, it could be God suggesting you pray for that person.

- People like to quote parts of the Bible to fit their own worldview. Never accept anything out of its proper context.

- People will often use, "Judge not lest ye be judged" to excuse their own or someone else's sinful behavior.

- Spiritual immaturity is a real problem, especially when it's all people settle for.

- Pray without ceasing really means keep the communication lines open and active. Sometimes you will just wait to hear.

- God loves you.